POPULAR CULTURE

A VIEW FROM THE PAPARAZZI

Orlando Bloom	John Legend
Kelly Clarkson	Lindsay Lohan
Johnny Depp	Mandy Moore
Hilary Duff	Ashlee and Jessica Simpson
Will Ferrell	
	Justin Timberlake
Jake Gyllenhaal	
Paris and Nicky Hilton	Owen and Luke Wilson
LeBron James	Tiger Woods

Johnny Depp

Jim Graziano

Mason Crest Publishers

Johnny Depp

FRONTIS
During his career Johnny Depp has become known for taking unusual film roles. Today he is one of America's favorite actors.

Produced by 21st Century Publishing and Communications, Inc.

MASON CREST PUBLISHERS INC.
370 Reed Road
Broomall, Pennsylvania 19008
(866) MCP-BOOK (toll free)
www.masoncrest.com

Printed in the United States.

First Printing

9 8 7 6 5 4 3 2 1

Library of Congress Cataloging-in-Publication Data

Graziano, Jim.
    Johnny Depp / Jim Graziano.
       p. cm.—(Pop culture: a view from the paparazzi)
    Includes bibliographical references and index.
    Hardback edition: ISBN-13: 978-1-4222-0200-5
    Paperback edition: ISBN-13: 978-1-4222-0354-5
    1. Depp, Johnny—Juvenile literature. 2. Motion picture actors and actresses—United States—Biography—Juvenile literature. I. Title.
PN2287.D39G73 2008
791.43'028092—dc22
[B]   2007012674

Publisher's notes:
- All quotations in this book come from original sources, and contain the spelling and grammatical inconsistencies of the original text.

- The Web sites mentioned in this book were active at the time of publication. The publisher is not responsible for Web sites that have changed their addresses or discontinued operation since the date of publication. The publisher will review and update the Web site addresses each time the book is reprinted.

CONTENTS

Johnny Depp won many new fans when he played Captain Jack Sparrow, the hero of Disney's 2003 film *Pirates of the Caribbean: The Curse of the Black Pearl*. The role of the strange but appealing pirate won Johnny his first Academy Award nomination, and he later played Captain Jack in two other Disney films.

1

Anything But a Curse

Over the years Johnny Depp's film characters have included a pale-faced young man with metal shears for hands (*Edward Scissorhands*), the wild journalist Hunter S. Thompson (*Fear and Loathing in Las Vegas*), and even a 17th-century poet (*The Libertine*). But his most famous role required Johnny to wear black eyeliner, gold teeth, and shells and trinkets in his hair.

For most of his fans, Johnny's performance as the swashbuckling Captain Jack Sparrow was the best part of the 2003 film *Pirates of the Caribbean: The Curse of the Black Pearl*. That movie was an enormous success, earning

7

over $650 million worldwide. Its 2006 **sequel**, *Pirates of the Caribbean: Dead Man's Chest*, earned more than $1 billion worldwide.

A Surprise Hit

When **producer** Jerry Bruckheimer received the original script for *Pirates of the Caribbean*, he was not very excited about the movie. Although he had hoped to get Johnny Depp to play the **lead**, Bruckheimer doubted the actor would be interested. After all, Johnny had made a career out of playing unique characters in unusual stories, and there have been dozens of movies made about pirates. However, when the script was rewritten Bruckheimer became more excited. He believed that adding mystical, ghostly aspects to the story was something that had not been done before.

Bruckheimer flew to France, where Johnny lives with his girlfriend Vanessa Paradis and their two young children, Lily-Rose and Jack, to try to convince him to star in the movie. The producer found Johnny excited about the project. He wanted to make a movie that his young children could enjoy, and he liked the idea of his children thinking of their father as a pirate.

Inspiration for a Pirate

Johnny has said that he modeled his character after Rolling Stones guitarist Keith Richards. In August 2003, he told *GQ* magazine in August 2003:

> **"I was . . . reading a lot of books about the pirates of that time, and these guys were absolutely without question the rock stars of that era. So I thought, 'Who's the greatest rock 'n' roll star?' Keith Richards. Keith is everything. He's so smooth, so brilliant. So he was a great inspiration for Jack."**

At first, the staff at Walt Disney Studios did not like the way Johnny was playing Captain Jack Sparrow. Disney was spending an enormous amount of money—approximately $125 million—to produce the film. Most of that was spent on the elaborate sets. For example, the cave where the evil Captain Barbossa hid his treasure took 100 craftsmen five months to build, and was eventually flooded with over 300,000 gallons of water. The Disney **executives** wanted to make sure that the Jack

Sparrow character was appealing, and at first they were not impressed with Johnny's performance. The actor later explained,

> **"There were a couple of high-end Disney executives who were fine with what I was doing, but there were a couple who were very worried, like, 'He's ruining the movie! Why is he acting like that? What's he doing with his hand?'"**

Johnny eventually asked the studio executives to either trust him or fire him. He was confident that the character would be appealing, and felt sure that in the end the studio would be happy with the finished product.

A Huge Hit

Johnny's instincts proved to be correct. When *Pirates of the Caribbean: The Curse of the Black Pearl* was released in 2003, it quickly became

Producer Jerry Bruckheimer (right) pauses for a photo with *Pirates of the Caribbean* costars Orlando Bloom (left) and Johnny Depp. Some Disney executives initially questioned Bruckheimer's decision to hire Johnny for a leading role in the film. However, it was clear that Bruckheimer had made the right choice when *Curse of the Black Pearl* became a huge international hit.

Johnny Depp greets a crowd of fans at a movie premiere. Johnny has always tried to take acting jobs that interest him, preferring unusual and quirky roles in independent films. He took the *Pirates of the Caribbean* job because he thought his children would enjoy seeing him as a pirate.

apparent that fans adored the mumbling, swaggering Captain Jack. Johnny noted that he was both "surprised" and "touched" by people's warm response to the film. Film critics liked the movie as well, with the well-known critic Roger Ebert writing:

"The movie made me grin, and savor the daffy plot, and enjoy the way Depp fearlessly provides a performance that seems nourished by deep wells of nuttiness."

As the film's earnings passed $100 million, then $200 million, Johnny began receiving phone calls from studio executives who wanted to congratulate him on the movie's success. He found it "deeply satisfying" when the people who had worried about the character a few months earlier were now telling him what a good job he had done.

Equally satisfying for Johnny was being nominated for his first Academy Award. The Oscar is one of the most prestigious awards an actor can receive, and Johnny said that he was surprised and honored to be nominated. Although Johnny didn't win the Oscar, he did win a Screen Actors Guild award for playing Captain Jack.

Doing Things His Way

Johnny has said that he appreciates all the praise from critics and from his peers. However, he is most interested in how his fans feel about the characters he plays. In November 2004, he told *Empire* magazine:

"Awards are not as important to me as when I meet a ten-year-old kid who says, 'I love Captain Jack Sparrow.' They were really affected by this character and took something away with them—that kid will have the memory in his head for a long time. That's real magic for me."

Having turned down starring roles in such blockbusters as *Speed*, *Interview with a Vampire*, and *Titanic*, it should come as no surprise that Johnny Depp is not impressed by film projects that are trendy or popular. From his childhood in Kentucky to his current status as one of America's greatest actors, Johnny has always done things his own way, never bothering to worry about what others think.

Johnny arrives with his mother, Betty Sue Palmer, at the 2004 Academy Awards ceremony in Hollywood. Johnny's childhood was turbulent, as his family moved often and his parents divorced when he was 15 years old. He has always had a very close relationship with his mother, and even has her name tattooed on his arm.

2

A Rocky Road

John Christopher Depp II was born on June 9, 1963. His father, John Depp Sr., was a civil engineer, while his mother, Betty Sue Palmer, was a waitress at a local coffee shop. Johnny had three older siblings: Danny (nicknamed "DP"), Debbie, and Christie. The Depp family lived in Owensboro, Kentucky, the third-largest city in the state.

Johnny had a close relationship with his mother—he has her name tattooed on his left arm—but his strongest relationship was with his grandfather, whom he called "Pawpaw." They spent a lot of time together. Johnny later said:

"We were inseparable, me and Pawpaw. He died when I was seven and that was a real big thing for me. But somehow I believe that he's still around— guiding, watching. I have close calls sometimes. I think . . . How did I get out of that? I've just got a feeling that it's Pawpaw."

Independent From the Start

Johnny's self-reliant spirit began to show itself early. He often resisted following rules and regulations that he considered silly, and this led to many clashes with authority figures. His first major conflict occurred in elementary school, when he was suspended for showing his buttocks to a teacher. This was the first in a long series of events that, years later, would result in Johnny dropping out of school.

After Johnny's grandfather died, the Depp family moved to Miramar, Florida, a small town just outside of Miami, where John Sr. took a job with the public works department. While there, the family lived in a series of hotel rooms and apartments. Johnny later said that he moved nearly 30 times. He eventually gave up trying to make new friends, because he knew his family would soon relocate to a new neighborhood.

Johnny was unhappy in Florida. At one point, to please his father, he agreed to play on a local football team. Johnny quit and rejoined the football team three times before he found something else that interested him: becoming a performer.

Watching his uncle, a minister who preached at a nearby church, inspired Johnny. Johnny liked the music of the gospel singers at the church, and enjoyed watching his uncle perform. He decided that he would like to entertain people when he grew up.

Rock 'n' Roll Roots

When Johnny was 12, his mother bought him an electric guitar for $25. After that, making music became an obsession. Johnny learned how to play his instrument by sitting in his room and strumming along to records. In a few years he started playing in a band called Flame with some local guys.

Unfortunately, around that time his rebellious behavior grew worse. The 14-year-old had started hanging out with some wild kids. He was doing drugs, stealing things, and skipping school. Some of his teachers warned Johnny that if he didn't change, he would end up in prison.

As a teenager Johnny hung around with a wild crowd, and as he grew older he always tried to be independent. However, Johnny rejects being labeled a rebel. "To me it was much more [about] curiosity," he told *Rolling Stone*. "It wasn't like I was some malicious kid. . . . I just wanted to find out what was out there."

"I'd been in high school three years. . . . I was bored out of my mind, and I hated it," Johnny later said, telling *Rolling Stone*:

> **"I did every kind of drug there was by fourteen, swiped a few six-packs, broke into a few classrooms, just to see what was on the other side of that locked door. Eventually you see where it's headed and you get out."**

Johnny later described his wild times in Miramar as a period of experimentation. Part of the problem may have been his unsettled home life. His parents divorced when Johnny was 15, and his father and sister Debbie moved to a different town.

In 1979, when Johnny was 16, he dropped out of school. He had started playing with a band called The Kids, which performed at local clubs. On average, each of the band members earned about $25 a night. A few times, the band made more, such as when they were the opening act for such famous music acts as the B-52s, Talking Heads, and Iggy Pop.

One of the band members introduced Johnny to his sister, Lori Ann Allison. A makeup artist who was five years older than Johnny, Lori Ann was also interested in a music career, although she wanted to be a recording engineer. The two set a goal to get The Kids signed to a record label. They also started dating, and were married in 1983, when Johnny was 20 years old.

Going to California

To make it big in the music business, The Kids decided to move to Los Angeles. They hoped to play in big clubs on the West Coast, where record company executives might notice the band. However, once they got to California The Kids had a hard time finding **gigs**. Johnny later recalled:

> **"It was horrible. There were so many bands it was impossible for us to make any money. So we all got side jobs. We used to sell ads over the telephone. . . . We had to rip people off. . . . It was horrible."**

Eventually Johnny and his bandmates decided things were not going to work out the way they had hoped. Around the same time, his marriage was breaking up. After two years of marriage, Johnny and Lori Ann decided to divorce.

When he was 12 years old, Johnny's mother bought him an inexpensive guitar, and the young boy dreamed of a career in music. Within a few years he was an accomplished guitarist and played in several bands. The 2001 movie *Chocolat* was the first film in which Johnny played guitar on screen.

A Lucky Break

Without a band or a job, Johnny desperately needed money. Luckily for him, before he and Lori divorced she had introduced him to a friend of hers named Nicolas Cage. Nicolas was an actor who had already appeared in several movies. He thought Johnny was good-looking

Director Wes Craven chose Johnny for a small part in his 1984 horror film *A Nightmare on Elm Street*. Johnny played the boyfriend of the film's heroine, and does not survive an attack by the evil Freddy Krueger. *Nightmare on Elm Street* was a huge hit, and helped Johnny realize that he could make a living as an actor.

enough to be a movie star, and convinced Johnny to meet with his **agent**. Johnny agreed, and soon he went an **audition**. Two days later he landed a part in the horror film *A Nightmare on Elm Street*.

In 1988 *Nightmare on Elm Street* **director** Wes Craven told *TV Guide* why he had hired the unknown and inexperienced actor for the film:

> **"He had a quiet charisma that none of the other actors had. Johnny . . . just had a very powerful, yet very subtle personality. My teenage daughter and her friends were at the reading, and they absolutely flipped out over him."**

Johnny was not on the screen for long—Freddy Krueger murders his character, Glen Lantz, during a nightmare. However, Johnny was very happy with his paycheck of $1,200 per week, and realized that although he still loved music he could make a living as an actor.

After taking a second movie role, in the teen comedy *Private Resort*, Johnny decided to get serious about acting. He enrolled in The Loft, a famous Los Angeles school for actors. Over the next few years he was occasionally offered acting jobs. He appeared in **episodes** of the television shows *Lady Blue* and *Hotel*, and had a part in a television movie called *Slow Burn*.

During one project, a short film being made by students at the American Film Institute called *Dummies*, Johnny met a young actress named Sherilyn Fenn. Laurie Frank, the director of *Dummies*, said the two fell madly in love. Months later Sherilyn and Johnny moved in together.

Making *Platoon*

In January 1986, Johnny received a copy of the script for *Platoon*, a movie about the experiences of a group of American soldiers during the Vietnam War. Oliver Stone, the director of *Platoon*, wanted Johnny to play the part of Private Gator Lerner, a military translator. Johnny was grateful to have the job.

Before Stone began filming *Platoon*, he made the actors undergo intense military-style training in the Philippines. The cast, which included Tom Berenger, Charlie Sheen, and Willem Dafoe, started the training by marching 60 miles (97 kilometers) from Manila into the dense jungle. While camped like soldiers, the actors had to fend off bugs and deal with bad weather and terrible food. This added to the stress of digging foxholes and constant military drills. Johnny later discussed the experience in a September 1988 interview with *Splice* magazine:

> **"We went through two weeks of training in the jungle in the Philippines. I gotta tell you, man, it was highly emotional. You put 30 guys in the jungle and leave them there to stay together for two weeks—just like a real platoon—and you build a real tightness. It's almost like a family. We became a military unit, a platoon."**

All of the cast's hard work paid off. *Platoon* was a huge hit, and was nominated for eight Academy Awards. The film won Oscars for Best Director, Best Film Editing, Best Picture, and Best Sound. Unfortunately, many of Johnny scenes were cut from the final film, so he did not wind up with much time on screen.

Becoming a Teen Idol

In 1987, producers from the fledgling Fox television network invited Johnny to audition for a new drama called *21 Jump Street*. Steve Beers, supervising producer of the show, later told *TV Guide*'s Elaine Warren:

> **"What struck me about [Johnny] when he auditioned was that he was not nervous. He was laid-back. He had this presence. He's an unusual personality. He's also one of the nicest people I've ever worked with."**

Johnny won the part of Officer Tom Hanson, a member of an undercover police squad. All of the squad members were young looking, and they worked in schools disguised as students, in order to prevent crimes. The show was based on the experiences of an actual police squad that had operated in Los Angeles schools during the early 1970s.

21 Jump Street became one of Fox's first hits. Johnny was a big part of the show's success—young fans, especially girls, loved his good-looking character. Soon Johnny was receiving some 10,000 fan letters a month, and was appearing on the covers of such teen magazines as *Tiger Beat* and *Bop*. In 1988 *Us* magazine named Depp one of the ten

MEMORIES OF GILDA • HOLLYWOOD'S DADS

SAY HOWDY TO *INDIANA JONES'* ALISON DOODY

VOLUME 3 NUMBER 105 $1.75/£1.50
JUNE 26, 1989

US

JUMP STREET'S
JOHNNY DEPP

HIS PRIVATE WORLD

The June 1989 issue of *US* magazine is just one of the many covers on which Johnny appeared when he was the star of *21 Jump Street*. The show was an early hit for Fox, running from 1987 until 1990. Johnny played Tom Hanson, a police officer who goes undercover to solve crimes in high schools.

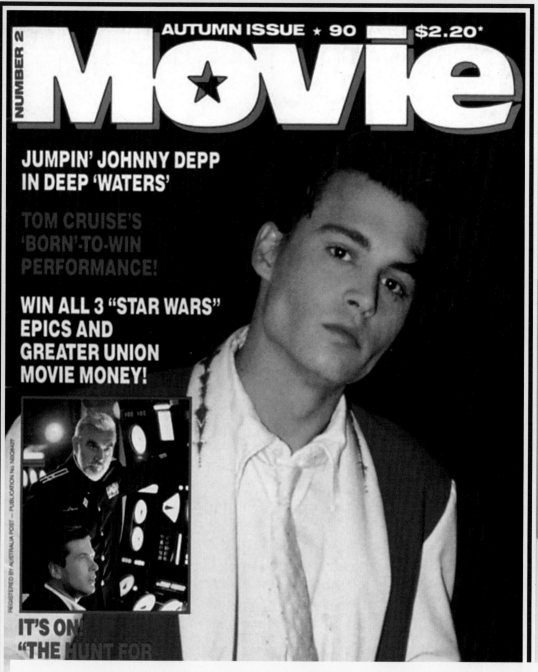

AUTUMN ISSUE ★ 90 $2.20*

NUMBER 2

M★vie

JUMPIN' JOHNNY DEPP
IN DEEP 'WATERS'

TOM CRUISE'S
'BORN'-TO-WIN
PERFORMANCE!

WIN ALL 3 "STAR WARS"
EPICS AND
GREATER UNION
MOVIE MONEY!

REGISTERED BY AUSTRALIA POST – PUBLICATION No. NBG9827

IT'S ON!
"THE HUNT FOR

Johnny was uncomfortable being called a teen idol for his work on *21 Jump Street*. "The earth was saturated with these horrific images of me as Tom Hanson," he later told *Rolling Stone*. "They'd invented this product, and this product somehow looked like me, and I had no control over it. . . . It feels really bad. It was horrible."

sexiest bachelors. However, Johnny was embarrassed at being idolized by young fans. He commented:

> **❝Those are things that are out of my control. It's very nice to be appreciated, but I'm not really comfortable with it. I've never liked being the center of attention.❞**

Johnny's lack of interest in his celebrity did not stop the media from talking about him. He began to worry that he would become **typecast**, and that he would only be appreciated for his looks and not his acting ability. Things began to get out of hand when the Fox network decided to take *21 Jump Street*'s stars on a tour of major U.S. cities. Johnny was overwhelmed by thousand of screaming fans clamoring for his autograph.

An Unhappy Star

By 1989 Johnny was tired of playing Tom Hanson. He began trying to disrupt the show, hoping to be fired. One day, he showed up to work with rubber bands wrapped around his tongue. Another time, he came onto the set wearing a turban and speaking in a funny accent. In 2003, he told *Entertainment Weekly*:

> **❝It was a frustrating time. I did not feel like I was doing anybody any good on there. Not them. Not the people watching the show. Certainly not myself. But at the time I tried to mask it by saying these were the choices I made for the character.❞**

The press reported stories about Johnny's strange behavior. Some news reports indicated that he had gotten a big head and was throwing temper tantrums on the set. In March 1989, tabloids reported that Johnny had been arrested for punching someone at a party. However, Johnny denied the rumors that he was hard to work with.

Johnny's personal life was also turbulent during this time. Although he had gotten engaged to Sherilyn Fenn, the constant separation caused by their busy work schedules took a toll on their relationship. The couple found themselves growing apart, and eventually separated. Johnny then started dating actress Jennifer Grey. The two soon became engaged, but broke up about six months after they had started dating.

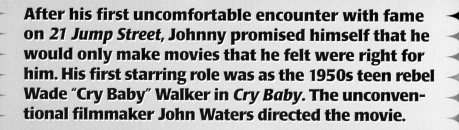

After his first uncomfortable encounter with fame on *21 Jump Street*, Johnny promised himself that he would only make movies that he felt were right for him. His first starring role was as the 1950s teen rebel Wade "Cry Baby" Walker in *Cry Baby*. The unconventional filmmaker John Waters directed the movie.

3

Getting Serious About Acting

In 1990 *21 Jump Street* finally ended, leaving Johnny free to pursue other acting jobs. One of his first new projects was a movie called *Cry Baby*. The director, John Waters, was known for his offbeat films. Waters planned to make *Cry Baby* a **parody** of teen movies like *Grease* or Elvis Presley's many films of the 1960s.

Johnny was excited at the opportunity to play the slick-haired Wade "Cry Baby" Walker, because it allowed him to poke fun at his heartthrob image. What better way to escape being a teen idol than to make fun of himself? He explained:

> **"Whenever a young actor comes out they have to pin him with some sort of label, so they call him 'bad boy' or they use that horrible word 'rebel.' It's all so played out and stupid. I just like to do roles which are interesting and cool. . . . That why I liked *Cry Baby*—it made fun of the teen idol stuff, the screaming girls."**

Overall, critics liked Johnny's performance in *Cry Baby*. However, the **musical** did not do well at the box office in the United States. *Cry Baby* only earned about $8 million in U.S. theatres, although it was more successful in foreign markets like Europe and Australia.

New Love, New Project

Johnny first saw actress Winona Ryder in 1989, when was getting a soda at the Ziegfield Theatre in New York City. She was in town for the premiere of her movie *Great Balls of Fire*. There was an immediate attraction between the two, although a mutual friend did not formally introduce Winona and Johnny until a few months later.

When Winona and Johnny first began dating, they did not know they would soon be working together on a film with director Tim Burton. Johnny met Burton in a New York City coffee shop, and later said of their first encounter that there was "an instant connection." Burton soon asked Johnny to audition for the leading role in his upcoming film *Edward Scissorhands*.

There was a lot of competition for the part—the movie studio was pressuring Burton to hire Tom Cruise, and such well-known young actors as Tom Hanks, Robert Downey Jr., and William Hurt were also interested. Even pop superstar Michael Jackson wanted the part of the Frankenstein-like teen with sharp blades for fingers. Burton, however, knew that Johnny was the right actor for the part.

Johnny was eager to try this different and challenging role. His strange character, with his pale, scarred skin and wild hair, was the complete opposite of a teen idol. Most people in the movie consider Edward a monster because of his appearance, and never bother to learn that he is kind-hearted and sensitive.

Wearing the costume of Edward Scissorhands, Johnny poses with his costar and girlfriend Winona Ryder. The film was a critical and commercial hit, with many reviewers praising Johnny's performance. "Johnny Depp plays Edward perfectly and Winona Ryder is excellent in a relatively small role as the cheerleader sweetheart," wrote James Welsh for *Films in Review*.

Winona played Kim, a girl who falls in love with Edward, while the famous horror film actor Vincent Price played Edward's wacky inventor. The weird but touching movie was a huge success both with the critics and at the box office. Johnny was nominated for his first major acting award, a Golden Globe for Best Performance by an Actor in a Musical or Comedy. *Edward Scissorhands* was the first of several award-winning movies Johnny would make with Burton—actor and director would later collaborate on such films as *Ed Wood*, *Sleepy Hollow*, and *Charlie and the Chocolate Factory*.

Career Opportunities

Johnny's relationship with Winona intensified while they were making *Edward Scissorhands*. He and Winona became engaged, and Johnny had the words "Winona Forever" tattooed on his right shoulder.

Johnny followed up his success in *Edward Scissorhands* with two film appearances in 1991. He made a **cameo** appearance in *Freddy's Dead: The Final Nightmare*, a movie in the Nightmare on Elm Street series. In the credits, Johnny was listed as "Oprah Noodlemantra." Other celebrities who appeared briefly in the film included comedians Rosanne Barr and Tom Arnold and rock star Alice Cooper.

Later that year, Johnny had a bigger part in the critically acclaimed film *Arizona Dream*. The movie also starred actress Faye Dunaway. Although *Arizona Dream* was praised widely in Europe, it was a flop in the United States.

Things Fall Apart

By the spring of 1993, the relationship between Winona and Johnny was ending. Their busy careers made it hard for them to spend time together, and speculation and rumors reported in the tabloids made their engagement unbearable. Winona later said:

> **"I remember us desperately hating being hounded. It was horrible and it definitely took its toll on our relationship. Every day we heard that we were either cheating on each other or were broken up when we were not. It was like this constant mosquito buzzing around us."**

After the breakup, Johnny was asked about his "Winona Forever" tattoo. In October 1993 he told *GQ* magazine:

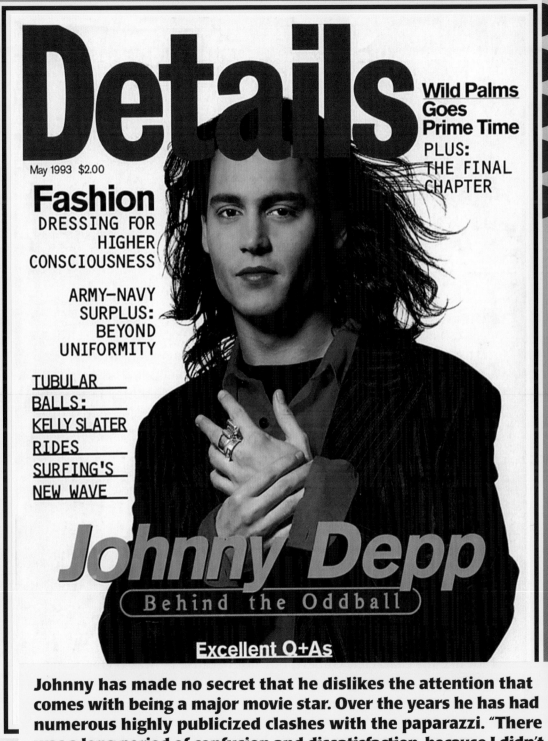

Details

May 1993 $2.00

Wild Palms Goes Prime Time

PLUS: THE FINAL CHAPTER

Fashion
DRESSING FOR HIGHER CONSCIOUSNESS

ARMY–NAVY SURPLUS: BEYOND UNIFORMITY

TUBULAR BALLS: KELLY SLATER RIDES SURFING'S NEW WAVE

Johnny Depp
Behind the Oddball

Excellent Q+As

Johnny has made no secret that he dislikes the attention that comes with being a major movie star. Over the years he has had numerous highly publicized clashes with the paparazzi. "There was a long period of confusion and dissatisfaction, because I didn't understand any of [the public interest]," he told *Newsweek* in 2006.

> **"I think of my tattoos like a journal and to have it removed, or erase it, is to try and say it never happened. We were together for three years and at the time, I really did think it would be forever."**

A little more than a year later, Johnny changed his mind and began the painful process of having part of the tattoo removed. Today it reads, "Wino Forever."

Quirky Characters

In Johnny's next few movies, he would continue to play strange characters. Preparing for the 1993 film *Benny and Joon* allowed Johnny to study the careers of two stars of the silent film era. In the movie, he played Sam, a quirky young man obsessed with Charlie Chaplin and Buster Keaton. Sam falls in love with Joon, a mentally disturbed young woman being looked after by her brother Benny.

Johnny's next film was *What's Eating Gilbert Grape*, in which he starred with Leonardo DiCaprio and Juliette Lewis. Johnny's character, Gilbert, is a young man with a lot of family problems who is stuck in a small town. His mother is so fat that she never leaves the house and his younger brother Arnie is mentally ill. Johnny later compared the fictional town where Gilbert lives to his own life in Miramar, Florida. He commented:

> **"Gilbert Grape would seem like a pretty normal kind of guy, but I was interested in what was going on underneath. . . . I understand the feeling of being stuck in a place. . . . I can understand the rage of wanting to completely escape from it and from everybody and everything you know and start a new life."**

Leonardo DiCaprio later told *Premiere* magazine that Johnny was a lot like his character, Gilbert, but not because he was trying to be that way:

> **"There's an element of Johnny that's extremely nice, and extremely cool, but at the same time, he's hard to figure out. But that's what makes him interesting."**

A publicity photo of the cast of *What's Eating Gilbert Grape*; Johnny is seated at the top left with (clockwise) Juliette Lewis, Darlene Cates, Mary Kate Schellhardt, Leonardo DiCaprio, and Laura Harrington. Johnny's character Gilbert narrates the 1993 film about a strange family that lives in a small Texas town.

Wild Times

In October 1993, around the time *Gilbert Grape* was released, a tragedy occurred. A young actor named River Phoenix, who was a friend of Johnny's, died of a drug overdose outside the Viper Room, a Los Angeles

American audiences did not like *Arizona Dream*, the first English-language production by the respected Bosnian filmmaker Emir Kusterica. However, foreign moviegoers and critics liked the film. In the British magazine *New Statesman and Society* Jonathan Romney wrote that *Arizona Dream* "is absolutely riveting; it works entirely on its own terms and no recognisable others."

club. Johnny was saddened by his friend's death. Because he was part-owner of the club, he also became upset when rumors began circulating that drugs were commonly used at the Viper Room.

In February 1994, Johnny was introduced to Kate Moss, a model from England. From the moment they met, the two were seemingly inseparable. Unfortunately, the tabloids were always watching the couple and reporting on their actions, just as they had when Johnny was dating Winona Ryder. Johnny found himself defending his petite girlfriend against allegations that she had an eating disorder. "Why punish someone because they have a good metabolism?" he commented. Sometimes, he got into arguments with paparazzi photographers who were following the couple.

Later that year Johnny was arrested after a disturbance at New York's posh Mark Hotel. While staying with Kate in a $500-a-night room at the hotel, he got into a disagreement with a hotel security guard. Johnny became so angry that he smashed up his hotel room. The police were called, and within a half an hour, three officers escorted the actor out of the building in handcuffs. Johnny ended up paying about $9,000 for everything he'd broken.

Another Hit Movie

While Johnny's personal life seemed to be a mess, his career was going just fine. In 1994 he teamed up with Tim Burton again. This time, the project was *Ed Wood*, a **biopic** about a movie director who had become known for making terrible films. Although *Ed Wood* did not make much money at the box office, it received wide critical acclaim. *Empire* magazine called Johnny's performance "mesmerizing," while *Premiere* magazine raved:

> **"Depp plays Wood as a wide innocent caught up in the illusions of cinema. He's another *Edward Scissorhands*. He looks petrified with glee throughout the film."**

Ed Wood won a pair of Oscars, and for his performance Johnny received his third Golden Globe nomination, for Best Actor in a Comedy.

Johnny experienced much personal turmoil during the mid-1990s. "That was kind of a nasty, darker period for me," he told *Rolling Stone* in 2005. "I can't say I was completely unhappy, but I couldn't get a grasp on it, so I spent years poisoning myself. . . . Now I look back and say, 'Why? Why did I do that?'"

4

What's Eating Johnny?

J ohnny needed a break from the pressure of fame. He found his outlet in music, and began playing guitar with a band called P. The band included some well-known musicians along with Johnny's childhood friend Sal Jenco. P soon signed a recording contract with Capitol Records and released its first album in November 1995.

Johnny has continued to enjoy making music, even though his main focus remains on his acting career. In 1997 he played a guitar solo on the Oasis song "Fade In-Out." The group's guitar player, Noel Gallagher, later said Johnny was "actually one of the best guitarists" he'd ever seen. Johnny has also played guitar in several of his movies, such as the 2000 film *Chocolat*. His songs appeared on the film's **soundtrack**. Three years later, he wrote and performed the song "Sands Theme," which was used in Robert Rodriguez's movie *Once Upon a Time in Mexico*. Johnny's character in that movie was a corrupt CIA agent, and "Sands Theme" played when his character first appeared.

A Busy Year

Johnny was busy throughout 1995, appearing in three films. He had the lead role in *Don Juan DeMarco*, playing a mentally disturbed young man who believed he was the world's greatest lover. While making this movie, Johnny had a chance to work with the legendary actor Marlon Brando, fulfilling a longstanding dream.

Johnny's next film was *Dead Man*, which was written and directed by his friend Jim Jarmusch. When he was writing the script, Jarmusch had Johnny in mind to play the lead character, a young man named William Blake. Blake wants to escape life in the city, so he travels to the Western frontier in the late 1800s, but ends up lost and dying in a place he does not understand. Jarmusch later had nothing but praise for his friend's work on *Dead Man*:

> **He is really one of the most precise and focused people I've ever worked with. The whole crew was kind of amazed by that. It's a side of him that I'm not really familiar with. I'm more familiar with seeing him fall asleep on the couch with the TV on all night. But it somehow fits; he's full of paradoxes.**

Johnny's next role was less quirky than most of his other characters. *Nick of Time* was a remake of Alfred Hitchcock's classic film *The Man Who Knew Too Much*. In the movie, Johnny played Gene Watson, an ordinary man who finds himself in the wrong place at the wrong time. Watson is in town with his young daughter attending his ex-wife's funeral. Christopher Walken is a villain who kidnaps Gene's daughter and threatens to kill her unless Watson assassinates a prominent politician. Gene is given a gun and 90 minutes to carry out the murder.

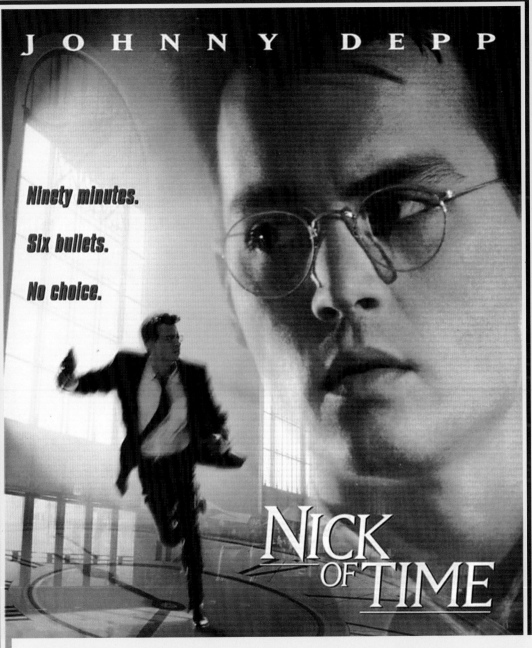

A promotional poster for Johnny's 1995 action film *Nick of Time*, in which his character must stop a political assassination plot. Kevin Thomas of the *Los Angeles Times* noted, "For Depp, the most venturesome young actor in Hollywood, *Nick of Time* represents a smart move into a genre that could expand his audience without diminishing his stature."

Moving Behind the Camera

Following *Nick of Time*, Johnny enjoyed a short break from work. Johnny and his brother, Dan, then began working together on a movie **screenplay**, which was based on a novel by Gregory MacDonald. This

Accompanied by girlfriend Kate Moss and rocker Iggy Pop, Johnny arrives at the 1997 Cannes Film Festival for the screening of *The Brave*, the first film he had directed. Despite the talented cast—Johnny's costar in the film is acclaimed actor (and close personal friend) Marlon Brando—*The Brave* was not well received by the Cannes audience.

would turn out to be *The Brave*, a film that marked Johnny's first time as a director. He also starred in the movie, playing a man who agrees to be murdered in order to earn money for his starving family. Critics in the United States did not like *The Brave*, but in 1997 it was nominated for the prestigious Palm D'Or ("Golden Palm") award at the Cannes Film Festival in France.

By the time Johnny arrived at the Cannes Film Festival, his paparazzi stalkers had began reporting that Johnny and Kate might not be dating anymore. The *New York Post* reported that their relationship was not going well, and that they had rented separate villas to occupy while they were in France. *New York* magazine said the pair had a "major break-up," while *People* reported that Moss wanted to "continue to date Depp." Despite the rumors, Johnny's spokesperson denied that the couple had broken up. Eventually, though, the actor admitted that his relationship with Kate was over.

Johnny's next film, *Donnie Brasco*, was based on the true story of an undercover FBI agent who worked to arrest members of organized crime families. Johnny described working with his costar, the award-winning actor Al Pacino, as "an honor" and "a real treat." He also worked hard to make his character believable. Joe Pistone, the real-life police officer whose adventures had inspired the story, said that Johnny had portrayed him perfectly.

Critics and fans all liked the film. The *Daily Star* wrote that *Donnie Brasco* was "the best gangster film since *The Godfather*." In *Rolling Stone*, critic Peter Travers wrote:

> **"Pacino and Depp are a match made in acting heaven, riffing off each other with astonishing subtlety and wit. Depp, an actor of admirable restraint, brings out the artful slyness in Pacino. The delicate balance of Depp's performance ranks him with the acting elite."**

Fear and Loathing

Johnnie's next major project was the 1998 film *Fear and Loathing in Las Vegas*. The movie was based on a novel by Hunter S. Thompson, a writer whose freewheeling, drug-influenced style of writing had become known as "gonzo journalism." Thompson's book was about a wild trip he and a friend took in the early 1970s to cover a motorcycle race in Las Vegas.

Johnny was excited about the project, as had become friends with Thompson three years earlier. He also admitted to being a fan of the book, telling a reporter:

> **[*Fear and Loathing*] was one of my favorite books since I was a kid. I remember reading it at seventeen and cackling like a banshee. I loved it! I went on to read the majority of Hunter's writing. When the idea came to do it as a film, I jumped at the chance.**

Everyone associated with the film—including Johnny, costar Benicio Del Toro, and director Terry Gilliam—was very pleased with the final result. However, the critics were less impressed. Most of the reviews were negative, and the film did poorly at the box office. That didn't stop Gilliam from praising Johnny's performance:

> **As far as I'm concerned, Johnny Depp is the best actor of his generation. I think he's capable of anything—there's no limit to his abilities. What amazes me is that the critics are always surprised by Johnny. . . . They don't understand how good an actor he is.**

More Movies

Filming for Johnny's next movie, *The Astronaut's Wife*, began in January 1998. In the movie Johnny plays Spencer Armacost, a NASA astronaut who briefly loses contact with headquarters while on a space mission. Armacost seems fine to most people when he returns from the mission, but his wife Jillian (played by Charlize Theron) notices that Spencer is not acting like the man she married. Her nightmares are plagued by strange visions and sounds. At first, Jillian is ecstatic when she finds out she is pregnant with twins. Soon, she begins to fear her husband is no longer human.

Johnny had long been committed to his next project, a movie called *The Ninth Gate*, and promptly began filming as soon as *The Astronaut's Wife* wrapped up. He was excited to work on *The Ninth Gate* with director Roman Polanski, and even reduced his usual fee in order to make the movie.

The Ninth Gate is based on a novel entitled *The Club Dumas*. Johnny played Dean Corso, a rare-book collector who is hired to

At a 1998 event in New York City, Johnny reads from *Fear and Loathing in Las Vegas*. He described the Hunter S. Thompson novel, about a drug-addled vacation taken by two friends during the early 1970s, as "one of my favorite books," and was very proud to star in the film version that was released in 1998.

find two copies of a mysterious text. Over the course of his search, Corso becomes trapped in an evil conspiracy that involves a centuries-old secret society of devil worshippers. Making the film was a lot of fun for Johnny, but he had no way of knowing that while filming *The Ninth Gate*, he would meet someone who would change his life.

Finding A Soulmate

Johnny was filming *The Ninth Gate* in Paris when he spotted a lovely French singer-songwriter named Vanessa Paradis at the Hotel Costes. For Johnny it was love at first sight. He told *Vanity Fair* in 2004, "I knew at that moment when she came up to me, I was ruined." That same year, he told *Ms. London* magazine:

> **"I pretty much fell in love with her the moment I set eyes on her. As a person, I was pretty much a lost cause at that point of my life. She turned all that around for me with her incredible tenderness and understanding. Very quickly, I realized I could not live without her. She made me feel like a real human being instead of someone Hollywood had manufactured. It sounds incredibly corny and phony, but that's exactly what happened to me and what she has meant to me."**

Vanessa was an accomplished singer, having released her first hit song, "Joe Le Taxi," 12 years earlier when she was just 14 years old. She was also an experienced actress. Her cinematic debut came in the 1989 film *Noce Blanch*, and her credits included such movies as *The Girl on the Bridge*, *Pleasure*, and *Half a Chance*. Vanessa also dabbled in fashion—she worked as a spokesmodel for the famous perfume company Coco Chanel, and had modeled for the fashion photographer Jean-Paul Goude.

Soon after Johnny and Vanessa met at the Hotel Costes, they decided to live together in an apartment located in Montmartre, an upscale section of Paris. Not long after that, Vanessa became pregnant and the couple bought a $2 million villa in a small town near Saint-Tropez in southern France. One thing Johnny liked about living in France was that he could find privacy there. Intense media attention had contributed to the failures of his relationships with Winona Ryder

Johnny and longtime girlfriend Vanessa Paradis are pictured at the 2004 Academy Awards ceremony in Los Angeles. Johnny has described the moment he saw Vanessa at the Hotel Costes in Paris: "Whammo, man, across the room, amazing, incredible, awesome." Today the couple spends much of their time at their villa in France.

Johnny and his three-year-old daughter Lily-Rose are pictured on a shopping trip at a California grocery store. Fatherhood "has given me everything," Johnny admitted to *People* magazine in 2003, while Vanessa Paradis told the French edition of *Elle*, "Johnny is a perfect father. He dresses the children, he changes them, he makes the children laugh."

and Kate Moss. Johnny was determined to keep Vanessa, and later his family, out of the spotlight.

Unfortunately, the actor still had occasional run-ins with the paparazzi. In 1999, Johnny and Vanessa were dining at Mirabelle, a fancy restaurant in London, when a small group of paparazzi showed up hoping to take pictures of Johnny's pregnant girlfriend. Johnny and Vanessa tried to leave through a side door in order to avoid the photographers, but the cameramen appeared as the couple was trying to get into their car. Johnny became angry and threatened the men with a short piece of wood, chasing them away. Because of the noise, the police showed up. They arrested Johnny and held him for 30 minutes, but he was eventually released without being charged or having to post bail.

Johnny Becomes a Father

Johnny and Vanessa's daughter, Lily-Rose Melody Depp, was born on May 27, 1999. The birth of his first child was very satisfying and rewarding for Johnny. He would later describe his life before Lily-Rose as "existing, but not living." In July 2003, he told *USA Weekend Magazine*:

> **"You cannot imagine the degree of joy and love and life that's available until you have a kid. I just did not get it."**

Almost three years later, Johnny and Vanessa had their second child: Jack John Christopher Depp III, born on April 10, 2002. By then, Johnny had really settled into life in the tiny French village. He enjoys living in a rural area and going to the local market to purchase fresh fruit and vegetables.

However, the newfound enjoyment of his personal life did not mean Johnny was finished making movies. He had decided that even though he worked in Hollywood, he did not have to deal with the madness that accompanies being a movie star. The family divides its time between their home near Saint-Tropez, their apartment in Paris, and Johnny's enormous mansion in Los Angeles.

Johnny and Vanessa pause and smile for photographers on November 16, 1999, the day the famous actor was honored with the 2,149th star on the Hollywood Walk of Fame. The stars, which honor celebrities for their contributions to the entertainment industry, are presented each year by the Hollywood Chamber of Commerce.

5

A
Pirate's Life

Because of his fondness for oddball characters and his distaste for the attention of the media, Johnny Depp has sometimes been called an "anti-Hollywood star." But in November 1999 the actor returned to Los Angeles for a special award—a star on the Hollywood Walk of Fame. The ceremony solidified his credentials as one of Hollywood's most important actors.

That year would also see the release of Johnny's most successful film to date, when he teamed up with Tim Burton for the third time. Their film *Sleepy Hollow* was loosely based on "The Legend of Sleepy Hollow," a famous short story by the 19th century American writer

Washington Irving. Johnny plays Ichabod Crane, but his character is very different from the character of the same name in Irving's story. In the movie, Crane is a detective who tries to use reason and modern technology to solve a supernatural mystery—a series of murders by a headless horseman.

Sleepy Hollow earned more than $200 million at the box office worldwide. The film and its stars also won several awards. Johnny was named Best Actor in the Horror category at the 2000 Blockbuster Entertainment Awards, and his costar Christina Ricci, won a Blockbuster award for Best Actress.

Parts Small and Big

In 2000 Johnny had small parts in several films. In the romantic *Chocolat*, he played a traveling guitar player. He had two small roles in *When Night Falls*, an award-winning movie about the Cuban poet Reinaldo Arenas. Although Arenas fought with Fidel Castro to overthrow the corrupt government of Cuba in 1959, he was eventually persecuted and jailed. Johnny played a Cuban military officer, as well as a person who helps smuggle one of Arenas's manuscripts out of prison. In *The Man Who Cried*, Johnny played a gypsy living in France during the 1940 invasion of Nazi Germany.

Johnny's next major film role was in the 2001 movie *Blow*. The movie was based on the real-life exploits of George Jung, who in the 1970s had brought cocaine to the United States from Colombia. While doing research for the role, Johnny went to the prison where Jung was being held. He wanted to find out what kind of person the drug dealer really was. Johnny later told interviewers that Jung was "smart," "charming," and a "victim of his upbringing." Johnny even said that if he had not become an actor, he might have wound up in prison like Jung.

Another of Johnny's movies released in 2001, *From Hell*, took a look at London's unsolved Jack the Ripper murders. During the 1880s five young prostitutes had been murdered in a brutal, ritualistic fashion in the city's Whitechapel district. In *From Hell* Johnny played a young, drug-addicted investigator trying to find the murderer. The film received good reviews, with the *New York Post* noting:

"[*From Hell* is] an instant classic. . . . The classiest and best-acted slasher movie of all time."

A scene from the 2006 Disney film *Pirates of the Caribbean: Dead Man's Chest*. The second film featuring Johnny as Captain Jack Sparrow was even more successful than the first, earning more than $1 billion internationally. A third film in the series, *Pirates of the Caribbean: At World's End*, was another huge hit when it was released in May 2007.

Captain Jack

Many of Jack's fans were surprised when they learned he would be playing the lead character in the Disney film *Pirates of the Caribbean*. After all, he had always made a career out of playing strange characters in quirky films, rather than starring in summer blockbusters. Johnny later explained that he had decided to make the movie because he wanted to do a film that his children would enjoy.

Producer Jerry Bruckheimer later explained why he wanted Johnny for the part of Captain Jack Sparrow:

"The way you get an audience to really embrace a movie is to cast against the grain. You find someone the audience would never expect to see in a Disney movie. I went after Johnny Depp. Johnny is an artist who's known to take on quirkier projects. He's a brilliant actor."

To make the film seem authentic, Johnny and many of the other actors had to perform stunts and sword fights. In one scene, Johnny even had to steer a large ship—something he'd never done before—while costar Orlando Bloom hoisted the sails. Johnny later said that the stunt work on *Pirates of the Caribbean* was the most challenging of his career.

The work paid off, as the finished film was a huge hit when it was released in 2003. Although some reviewers complained that the movie was too long, nearly everyone appreciated Johnny's performance as Captain Jack. In the Washington Post, critic Ann Hornaday wrote:

> **"Depp is the single best reason to see *Pirates of the Caribbean* if you're past the age of ten."**

In addition to receiving his first Oscar nomination, and winning a Screen Actors Guild award, Johnny was nominated for Best Actor awards by the British Academy of Film and Television Arts (BAFTA), the Golden Globes, and the Online Film Critics Society. Johnny was also named "Sexiest Man of 2003" by *People* magazine, and in 2004 *Rolling Stone* selected the actor as one of its "People of the Year."

Another Oscar Nomination

Johnny was nominated for a second Best Actor Oscar for his performance in the 2004 film *Finding Neverland*. In the movie he portrayed the Scottish playwright J.M. Barrie, the author of the classic children's tale *Peter Pan*. Playing Barrie proved to be particularly challenging, as Johnny had to master a Scottish accent. With the help of a dialect coach and some Scottish crewmembers, he was able to pull it off.

Finding Neverland, which is based on a play called *The Man Who Was Peter Pan*, was filmed in London. This made Johnny happy because it was not far from his home in France. Vanessa, Lily-Rose, and Jack came to the set to watch Johnny making the movie.

Another of Johnny's 2004 films, *The Libertine*, was definitely not appropriate for children. His character, John Wilmot, the Earl of Rochester, was no role model. Although Wilmot had been a brilliant poet and a naval hero of the 17th century, he was a drunken womanizer who had been banished from the royal court because of his obscene rhymes, and died from liver disease when he was 33.

That same year, Johnny starred with John Turturro in *Secret Window*, which was based on a Stephen King story. In the film Johnny's character,

Johnny received his second Academy Award nomination for 2004's *Finding Neverland*, in which he played J.M. Barrie, the British author who wrote the classic children's book *Peter Pan*. The film was nominated for seven Oscars, winning one. Johnny would later work with one of his young *Neverland* costars, Freddie Highmore, in *Charlie and the Chocolate Factory*.

Mort Rainey, is an author who moves to a rural area after being divorced. He is trying to write a novel, but is slowly losing his mind while being tormented by a strange man, played by Turturro, who claims Rainey has stolen from one of his own works.

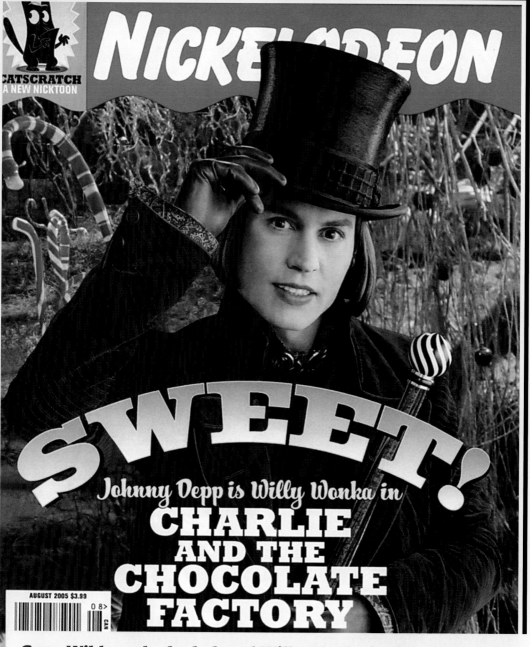

Gene Wilder, who had played Willy Wonka in the original film adaptation of Roald Dahl's book, made this comment when he learned that Tim Burton was creating a new version: "If I were going to cast the movie, I would cast Johnny Depp as Willy Wonka because I think he is wonderful. Mysterious—always—and magical."

Remaking Charlie

Johnny told *Rolling Stone* that getting the chance to play Willy Wonka in a remake of the film *Charlie and the Chocolate Factory* was the best present he'd gotten in 2005. For the fourth time, he would be collaborating with Tim Burton. The earlier version of the film, made in 1971, was generally considered one of the best children's movies of all time. The challenge for the director and his lead actor was to make their movie different, but still stay true to the original story, which had been written by children's author Roald Dahl. Burton later commented:

> **"I think just having Johnny in the film gives it a different spin. . . . I love working with him. . . . He always surprises me."**

Once again, both critics and fans liked the film. Most reviews were positive, and the movie was one of the year's biggest hits, earning more than $150 million. For the great job he did playing Willy Wonka, Johnny received a 2006 Teen Choice Award for Choice Actor in a Comedy.

Three months after *Charlie* was released, Johnny collaborated with Burton again, this time lending his voice to a character in the animated film *The Corpse Bride*. Johnny also attended the funeral of his friend Hunter S. Thompson. On August 20, 2005, approximately 280 people watched as Thompson's remains were fired out of a cannon, just as the author had wished. Johnny told the Associated Press that he was just trying to send his friend out "the way he wants to go out."

What the Future Holds

The success of 2006's *Pirates of the Caribbean: Dead Man's Chest* cemented Johnny's status as one of America's greatest actors. He signed on for another *Pirates* sequel, which was released in May 2007, and has said that he would be willing to make more films as the rum-swilling pirate. In fact, he enjoyed filming in the Caribbean so much that he and Vanessa bought a small island in the Bahamas.

Johnny's upcoming films include *The Rum Diary*, another movie based on a book by Hunter S. Thompson. He will also team up with Tim Burton for a sixth time on *Sweeney Todd*, a musical about a serial killer in 19th-century England. In another project, *Shantaram*, Johnny will play a bank robber who escapes from an Australian prison and lives in India and Afghanistan during the 1970s and early 1980s.

Johnny explains his career choices this way: "If I was going to do something, it had to be on my terms—not because I'm some hideous control freak—but because I don't want to live a lie. You really don't want to look back on your life and go, 'I was a complete fraud.'"

Undoubtedly, Johnny will also continue doing charitable work. He began trying to use his fame to help others in the late 1980s, when he was starring on *21 Jump Street*. At that time he directed several television ads for a child-abuse hotline and became involved in the Make-A-Wish Foundation, which helps children who are suffering from terminal illnesses. In October 2006 Johnny received the Courage to Care Award, honoring his commitment to children's charities, at a benefit event for the Los Angeles Children's Hospital.

In 2004, after the enormous success of *Pirates of the Caribbean: The Curse of the Black Pearl*, Johnny explained the reasons he felt that his career had succeeded:

> **"I was in it for the long haul. I decided early on to be patient and wait for the roles that interested me, not the roles that would advance my career. I never wanted to be remembered for being a star."**

Whatever the future holds for Johnny Depp, both his fans and critics can expect to see him do things his way and on his own terms—just as he always has.

1963 John Christopher Depp II is born on June 9 in Owensboro, Kentucky.

1971 The Depp family moves to Miramar, Florida.

1975 Johnny's mother, Betty Sue, buys him his first guitar. It is not long before he begins playing in bands.

1979 Johnny drops out of high school to pursue a music career.

1983 Depp marries Lori Ann Allison. They divorced two years later.

1984 Johnny makes his film debut with a small part in Wes Craven's *A Nightmare on Elm Street*.

1986 After almost giving up on a career in acting, Johnny lands a role in *Platoon*.

1987 The new Fox television show, *21 Jump Street*, premiers with Johnny as one of the three stars.

1990 Johnny attempts to shed his teen idol image by starring in two offbeat roles—*Cry Baby* and *Edward Scissorhands*. He begins dating Winona Ryder.

1993 Johnny is praised for his acting in *What's Eating Gilbert Grape?* and *Benny and Joon*. He breaks up with Winona Ryder and begins dating Kate Moss.

1994 Johnny reunites with Tim Burton to make *Ed Wood*. In September, Johnny is arrested for destroying a room at the Mark Hotel.

1995 Johnny's band P releases an album on Capitol Records. Johnny appears in three films: *Don Juan DeMarco*, *Dead Man*, and *Nick of Time*.

1996 Johnny directs his first full-length film, *The Brave*, after cowriting the screenplay with his brother, Dan. He receives rave reviews for his performance in *Donnie Brasco*.

1997 Johnny ends his relationship with Kate Moss.

1998 While filming *The Ninth Gate* in France, Johnny meets singer-songwriter Vanessa Paradis. The two begin dating and soon move into an apartment together. *Fear and Loathing in Las Vegas* is released.

1999 Vanessa and Johnny's first child, Lily-Rose Melody Depp, is born on May 27. *Sleepy Hollow* is released.

2000 Johnny appears in *Before Night Falls* and *Chocolat*.

2001 *Blow* and *From Hell* are released.

2002 Jack John Christopher Depp III is born on April 10.

2003 *Pirates of the Caribbean: The Curse of the Black Pearl* becomes a major international hit, and Johnny's most successful film to date. He also stars in Robert Rodriguez's film *Once Upon a Time in Mexico*.

2004 Johnny receives his first Academy Award nomination, for Best Actor in *Pirates of the Caribbean: The Curse of the Black Pearl*. He appears in *Finding Neverland*, *The Libertine*, and *Secret Window*.

2005 Tim Burton and Johnny reunite for the remake of *Charlie and the Chocolate Factory*.

2006 *Pirates of the Caribbean: Dead Man's Chest* earns over $1 billion worldwide.

2007 The third film in the *Pirates of the Caribbean* series, *At World's End*, opens in May.

Filmography

1984 *A Nightmare on Elm Street*
1985 *Private Resort*
1986 *Slow Burn; Platoon*
1990 *Cry Baby; Edward Scissorhands*
1991 *Freddy's Dead: The Final Nightmare; Arizona Dream*
1993 *What's Eating Gilbert Grape?; Benny and Joon*
1994 *Ed Wood*
1995 *Don Juan DeMarco; Dead Man; Nick of Time*
1996 *Donnie Brasco; The Brave; Cannes Man*
1998 *LA Without a Map; Fear and Loathing in Las Vegas*
1999 *The Astronaut's Wife; The Ninth Gate; Sleepy Hollow*
2000 *The Man Who Cried; Before Night Falls; Chocolat*
2001 *Blow; From Hell*
2003 *Pirates of the Caribbean: The Curse of the Black Pearl; Once Upon a Time in Mexico*
2004 *Finding Neverland; The Libertine; Secret Window; Happily Ever After* (French film)
2005 *Tim Burton's Corpse Bride; Charlie and the Chocolate Factory*
2006 *Pirates of the Caribbean: Dead Man's Chest*
2007 *Sweeney Todd; Pirates of the Caribbean: At World's End*
2008 *Shantaram*

Awards and Award Nominations

1990 ShoWest Award, Male Star of Tomorrow

nominated, Golden Globe Award, Best Actor in a Musical or Comedy (*Edward Scissorhands*)

1993 nominated, Golden Globe Award, Best Actor in a Musical or Comedy (*Benny and Joon*)

1994 nominated, Golden Globe Award, Best Actor in a Musical or Comedy (*Ed Wood*)

1996 London Critics Circle Film Award, Actor of the Year (*Ed Wood* and *Don Juan DeMarco*)

1998 Golden Aries (Russian Guild of Film Critics), Best Foreign Actor (*Fear and Loathing in Las Vegas*)

1999 Screen Actors Guild, star awarded on Hollywood Walk of Fame at 7020 Hollywood Boulevard

César Awards, France, honorary award

2000   Blockbuster Entertainment Awards, Favorite Male Actor—Horror (*Sleepy Hollow*)

2003   Screen Actors Guild Awards, Outstanding Performance by a Male Actor in a Leading Role (*Pirates of the Caribbean: The Curse of the Black Pearl*)

2004   MTV Movie Award, Best Male Performance (*Pirates of the Caribbean: The Curse of the Black Pearl*)

IFTA Award, Best International Actor

Teen Choice Awards, Choice Movie Fight/Action Scene and Choice Movie Liar (*Pirates of the Caribbean: The Curse of the Black Pearl*)

nominated, Golden Globe, Best Actor in a Musical or Comedy (*Pirates of the Caribbean: The Curse of the Black Pearl*)

nominated, Academy Award, Best Actor (*Pirates of the Caribbean: The Curse of the Black Pearl*)

nominated, BAFTA, Best Actor (*Pirates of the Caribbean: The Curse of the Black Pearl*)

nominated, People's Choice Award, Favorite Male Movie Star

2005   People's Choice Award, Favorite Male Movie Star

nominated, Golden Globe Award, Best Actor in a Drama (*Finding Neverland*)

nominated, Academy Award, Best Actor (*Finding Neverland*)

nominated, Screen Actors Guild Awards, Outstanding Performance by a Male Actor in a Leading Role (*Finding Neverland*)

2006   Teen Choice Award, Choice Movie Actor—Drama/High Adventure (*Pirates of the Caribbean: Dead Man's Chest*)

People's Choice Award, Favorite Male Movie Star

2007   People's Choice Awards, Best Male Actor and Favorite Male Action Star (*Pirates of the Caribbean: Dead Man's Chest*)

nominated, Golden Globe, Best Actor in a Musical or Comedy (*Pirates of the Caribbean: Dead Man's Chest*)

nominated, Kids' Choice Award, Favorite Male Movie Star

Books

Bingham, Jane. *Johnny Depp*. Chicago: Raintree, 2006.

Goodall, Nigel. *The Secret World of Johnny Depp: The Intimate Biography of Hollywood's Best Loved Rebel*. London: John Blake Publishing, 2006.

Johnstone, Nick. *Johnny Depp: The Illustrated Biography*. London: Carlton Publishing Group, 2006.

Meikle, Denis. *Johnny Depp: A Kind Of Illusion*. London: Reynolds & Hearn, 2005.

Pomerance, Murray. *Johnny Depp Starts Here*. Piscataway, N.J.: Rutgers University Press, 2005.

Web Sites

www.deppimpact.com

A Web site with information about Johnny, including a brief bio, a list of his films, and links to numerous interviews.

www.imdb.com

The Internet Movie Database contains information and reviews of thousands of films, as well as information about people in the movie industry and movie news.

www.imdb.com

The Internet Movie Script Database has hundreds of scripts available for free perusal and download.

www.rollingstone.com

The Internet version of *Rolling Stone* magazine contains hundreds of interviews as well as music and movie reviews.

www.salon.com

This online magazine covers a variety of topics, from politics to pop culture.

agent—the person responsible for the business dealings of an actor, writer, director, or artist. Agents often recommend roles for their clients and arrange auditions.

audition—an interview for a role or job as an actor, musician, or other type of entertainer.

biopic—a combination of the words "biography" and "picture," used to describe a film that is based on a person's life story.

cameo—a small appearance in a film or television show, generally used to describe an appearance by an actor who would not normally play such a minor part.

director—the person in charge of guiding the actors in their performances, coordinating filming, and who usually has a lot of influence on the final film.

episode—each of a series of segments presented in a television or radio show.

executive—a senior manager in a company or organization who is responsible for making and implementing decisions.

gig—a performance by a musician or group, usually at a place where the performer(s) do not regularly appear.

lead—the starring role in a film, television program, or radio show.

musical—a film or play in which singing and dancing play a major part.

parody—an imitation of a particular style of film, music, or art, often using exaggeration for comic effect.

producer—the person responsible for hiring actors to work on a movie, obtaining financing, and making sure the film is made.

screenplay—the script of a movie, including scene directions and instructions for the actors.

sequel—a published, broadcast, or recorded work that continues a story that began in a previous work, generally by using many of the same characters and possibly introducing some new ones.

soundtrack—the musical accompaniment for a film or television show.

typecast—this occurs when an actor always plays characters who are similar, so that he becomes associated with that character and is overlooked for other, different parts.

ABOUT THE AUTHOR

James Graziano is a musician who attended New York University. He currently resides in central New Jersey, touring and playing with his band, The Frantic. This is his first book.

Picture Credits

page

2: imkoxng-21/Inf/Goff
6: Walt Disney Pictures/NMI
9: Newswire Photo/NMI
10: Reuters Photo Archive
12: WENN Photos
15: Fox/UPI Archive
17: Miramax Films/NMI
18: KRT/MCT
21: New Millennium Images
22: New Millennium Images
24: Universal Pictures/NMI
27: 20th Century Fox/NMI
29: New Millennium Images

31: Paramount Pictures/NMI
32: Warner Bros. Pictures/KRT
34: KRT/MCT
37: Paramount Pictures/NMI
38: Patrick Hertzog/AFP
41: Stephen Trupp/StarMax
43: KRT/MCT
44: London Entertainment/Splash
46: Russ Einhorn/StarMax
49: Walt Disney Pictures/NMI
51: Miramax Films/NMI
52: New Millennium Images
54: Abaca Press

Front cover: Hahn/Khayat/Abaca Press/KRT
Back cover: Walt Disney Pictures/NMI